LOOK AT
HANDS

Franklin Watts
12a Golden Square
London W1R 4AB

Franklin Watts Australia
14 Mars Road
Lane Cove
N.S.W. 2066

ISBN 0 86313 554 4

Design: David Bennett
Illustrations: Julia Osorno

Printed in Italy
by G. Canale & C. S.p.A. Turin

The author and publisher would
like to thank the following people
for their participation in the
photography of this book:
Aman and Kavita Arora, Tyrone Watkins,
James Green, Nicola Hickamann-Robertson,
Alexandra Cragg, Leo Thomson, Sarah
Knight, Melissa Case, Chloe Thomson,
Sara Berman, Sonya Obrart, Zurki
Lily Ridett, Rosie Lewis, Ursula Hageli
of the Royal Ballet, Rosa Curling.

Additional photographs:
Chris Fairclough: page 21 (top left and bottom);
Science Photo Library: page 7;
John Watney: page 22; Zefa: page 21 (top right)

Illustration page 23 © National Deaf Children's
Society 1986. Drawn by Stephen Iliffe.

LOOK AT
HANDS

Ruth Thomson
Photography by Mike Galletly

FRANKLIN WATTS
London · New York · Sydney · Toronto

What can you tell about people from seeing only their hands? Who is a child or a grown-up? Who is male or female?

Hands are probably
the busiest part of your body.
Think how many different ways
you can move them.

Can you move each finger
on its own? Can you bend them
both forwards and backwards?
What can your thumb do
that your fingers can't?

This is what you would see
if you could see inside your hand.

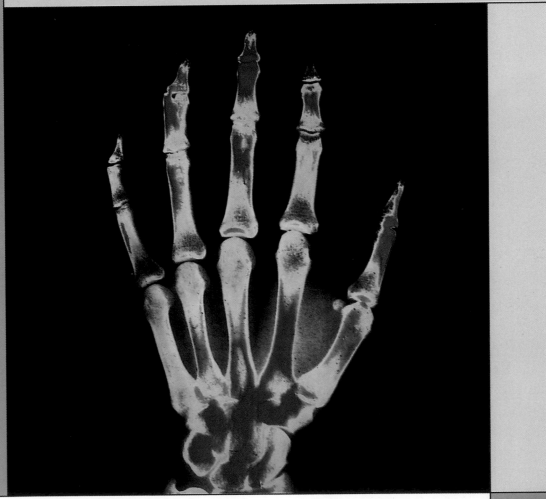

Count how many bones
there are. Why do you think
there are so many?

Look closely at your palm.
It is covered with tiny ridges.
These help you to grip.

Look particularly at the ridges
on your fingertips.
No-one in the whole world
has identical patterns.
The three basic patterns are
loops, whorls and arches.
Which of these do you have?

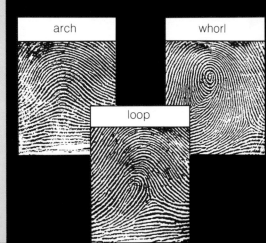

arch

whorl

loop

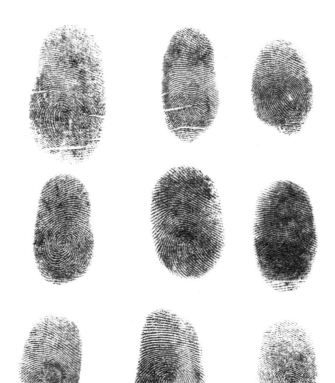

Which of these fingerprints matches this one?

Using an ink pad, let everyone in your group make two thumb prints. Name one and number the other. Display the numbered ones and see how many of the named prints you can match.

Hands are very useful.
You can use them in so many ways...

to squeeze

to grip

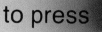

to press

to twist

to pull

Your thumb is especially useful because it can move across your hand and press against your fingers.
This makes it easy to hold objects of any shape or size.
Only human hands can do this.

Try doing any of these things
without using your thumb.
How well can you manage?
Think what you do using only
a thumb and first finger.

How do you use your hands
to play with these objects?

Your fingertips are sensitive. They help protect you from danger by warning you of pain and heat.

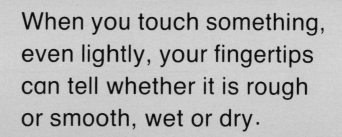

When you touch something, even lightly, your fingertips can tell whether it is rough or smooth, wet or dry.

Put objects with different
textures into a bag.
Invite a friend to put her
hand in the bag and feel the
objects one at a time.
Ask your friend to describe
how each one feels,
and to guess what
each one is.

People can use their hands
to talk –

to say hello

or goodbye...

to show anger

or joy.

19

What do you think these people are saying with their hands?

Sometimes, the same gesture can have different meanings. What do these gestures mean?

21

Deaf people can talk to one another using their hands.

Here are some deaf signs.
Can you use them to talk
to a friend?

 There's

 the...

bed

box

door

boy

dinner

rug

wardrobe

piano

Dancers use their hands to mime a story and to express their feelings.

'If a man promises to **love** me ▶

and **marry** me ▼

and **swears** to be faithful... ▶

I

shall be a **swan**

no more.'

This dance mime comes
from a ballet called
Swan Lake.

Have fun with your hands.
Shine a spotlight against a wall
in a darkened room and make
some funny shadow shapes.

Paint animal faces on your hands and give a puppet show.

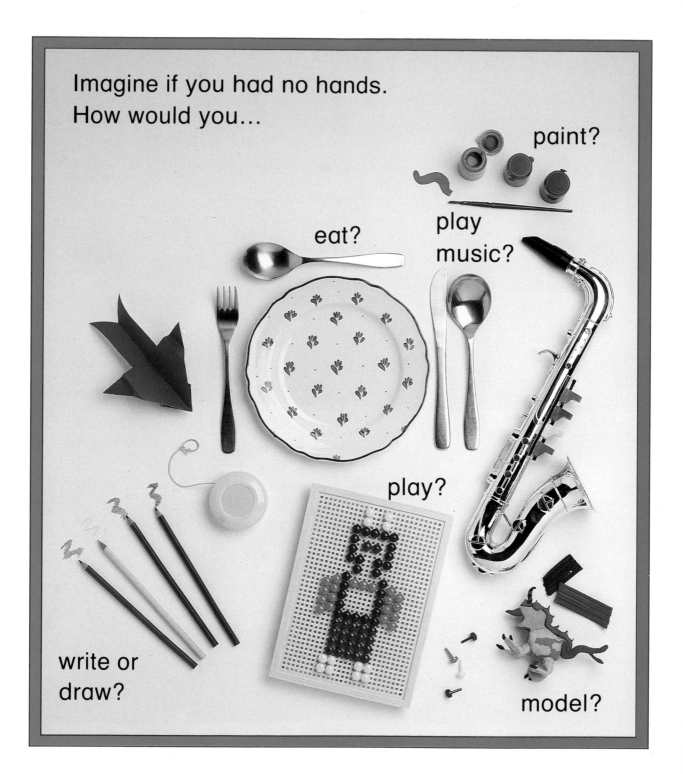

Imagine if you had no hands.
How would you…

paint?

eat?

play music?

play?

write or draw?

model?

28

Do you know?

● You have more than 25 bones in each hand. There are 8 small bones at the wrist joint. These little bones allow you to make small, quick movements. The bones in the fingers are joined in two places, which enables your fingers to bend. Your two hands contain more than a quarter of the total number of bones in your body.

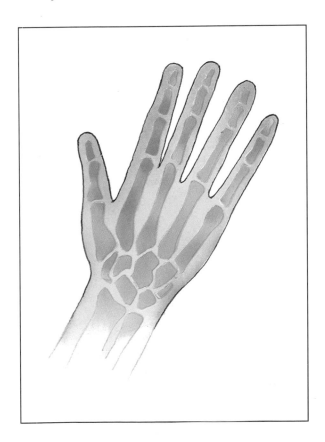

● The palms of your hands (and the soles of your feet) produce much more sweat than the rest of your body. The sweat helps your hands to grip.

Wash and dry your hands very thoroughly and then try to pick up something tiny. Do you find it easier if your hands are slightly damp?

● The palms of your hands and the soles of your feet are the only parts of your body which never tan in the sunshine.

● Your fingernails are formed from skin. The nails themselves are dead. The only living parts are the roots. A substance called keratin in the top layer of skin causes the nails to harden.

● Fingernails provide a hard base for the skin of your fingertips to push against. This helps their sensitivity to touch.

● 19 out of 20 people are right-handed. Which are you – right or left-handed?

Things to do

● Test how sensitive your sense of touch is. Collect all sorts of paper, such as tissue paper, newspaper, writing paper, wrapping paper, tissues, sugar paper and brown paper. Shut your eyes and see how many you can identify by feeling them.

● Now find flat objects with very different textures, such as some sandpaper, a flannel, some cloth, a mirror, a woolly glove, some wood and a tile. Shut your eyes and lightly touch each surface with your fingertips. Describe the textures that you feel.

● Cross the first and second fingers of one hand. Now feel a bead or a marble with those fingers. You should be amazed to find that you can feel not one, but two beads!

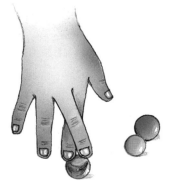

● You will need three bowls of water for this experiment – one hot (but not too hot to touch comfortably), one cold and one icy.

Put one hand in the hot water and the other in the icy water and leave them there for a minute or so. Then put both hands in the cold water. How does each hand feel now?

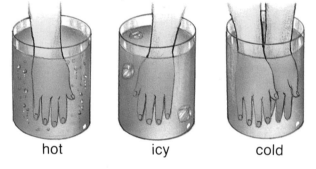

hot   icy   cold

● Early measurement were based upon the relationship between various parts of the body.

The main standard of length was the cubit – the length of the forearm from the elbow to the tip of the middle finger.

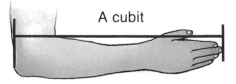

A cubit

There were also smaller measures based upon the hand:

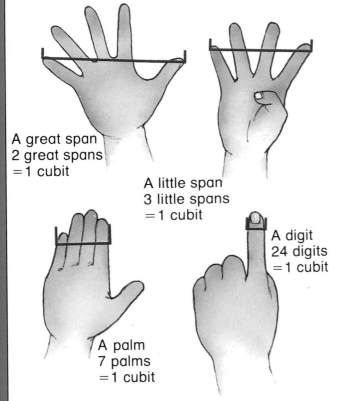

A great span
2 great spans
= 1 cubit

A little span
3 little spans
= 1 cubit

A palm
7 palms
= 1 cubit

A digit
24 digits
= 1 cubit

See for yourself. Using a piece of string, measure the length from your middle finger to your elbow and cut the string.

Use your cubit string to measure a table, a window or a door. Use the smaller measures as well. Compare your measurements with those of your friends. Are they the same?

Words about hands

The word *hand* is used in many different ways. Can you find out what these words mean?

handy
handful
hand-me-down
handout
handpick
handrail
handicraft

handhold
handyman
handcuffs
handcart
handmade
handtool

Sayings about hands

How many of these sayings do you know? What do they mean?

Many hands make light work.
A bird in the hand is worth two in the bush.
Lend a hand.
Keep your fingers crossed!
To win hands down.
To live from hand to mouth.
To be light-fingered.
To get the upper hand.
To wash one's hands of something.
To slip through one's fingers.
To be a dab hand.
To get out of hand.
To have fingers in many pies.

Index